THE ENGLISH POETS IN PICTURES
EDITED BY DOROTHY WELLESLEY

BYRON

BYRON
Oil painting by West

By courtesy of the Headmaster of Harrow School

BYRON

With four colour plates & twenty
black and white illustrations

Published for
PENNS IN THE ROCKS PRESS
by
WILLIAM COLLINS OF LONDON
MCMXXXXI

The Editor is most grateful to all those who have
so kindly helped in the selection of illustrations
and to all those who have so generously
allowed pictures and MSS. to be repro-
duced, special thanks being due to
officials of the public Museums,
Libraries and Galleries.

69705

821
BYR

PRODUCED BY ADPRINT LIMITED LONDON W I

PRINTED IN GREAT BRITAIN

LIST OF ILLUSTRATIONS

COLOUR PLATES

BLACK AND WHITE ILLUSTRATIONS

BLACK AND WHITE ILLUSTRATIONS

The ornaments in this book have been reproduced from the first edition of Byron's 'Fugitive Pieces,' printed in 1806

BYRON
Engraving after a miniature

GEORGE GORDON NOEL, sixth Lord Byron, of Newstead Abbey in Nottingham, was born in London in 1788. His father died when he was three years old. Byron's mother was a woman of violent temper, who alternately spoilt and ill-treated her son, calling him " a lame brat " because of the slight deformity of his foot, an affliction with which he was born. His boyhood was spent mainly in Aberdeen in comparative poverty, until, at the age of ten, he succeeded to the peerage on the death of a great-uncle. He was educated at Harrow, where, in spite of his lameness, he developed a passion for athletics : later, he

7

entered Trinity College, Cambridge, and, while at that University, published his first volume of poems. These were fiercely attacked by the most famous literary journals of the day, the *Quarterly* and the *Edinburgh Review*, and for the rest of his life the poet and the reviewers were at open war. Byron wrote many satires on this subject, the chief of which is *English Bards and Scotch Reviewers*. In 1815 he married Anne Isabella, later called Annabella, daughter of Sir Ralph Milbanke. This marriage was, from the day of the wedding, a tragedy for both concerned. In 1816, after a separation from his wife, Byron left England. He spent much of his time in Italy, often with his friend the poet Shelley, with whom he formed perhaps one of the few sincere friendships of his life. In 1823 he sailed for Greece to take part in the struggle for Greek independence. The following year he died at Missolonghi.

Byron was in every sense that which the French call *âme damnée*. His friend Trelawny described him as having the head of an Apollo and the foot of a satyr. His romantic adventures with women are famous ; but it seems certain that his one enduring love was for his half-sister Augusta Leigh, by whom he had a daughter Medora. His personal beauty, the effect of his magnetism upon others, men and women alike, his vanity, his cruelty, the almost insane folly of his life, present many problems to the psychologist. But by the nobility and tragedy of his death in the swamps of Misso-

NEWSTEAD ABBEY

An engraving of Byron's home near Nottingham

longhi he regained all that he had sold to Mephistopheles.

The reason for his extraordinary popularity as a poet on the Continent of Europe remains something of a mystery to the English reader. Romantic rhetoric was the fashion of the age ; yet the greatest poets, such as Wordsworth and Shelley, escaped it. Their romantic outpourings were almost always controlled by thought. The frequent insincerity of Byron's sentiments, combined with the inferior poetic technique of his lyrics, harmed him in his native land. In his dramatic poems, such as "Childe Harold" or "Manfred," the magnificent power of his oratory obscures the fact that his thought remains commonplace. "Manfred" is perhaps the finest of his longer poems, for here we enter the mysterious atmosphere that still surrounds the man. As the poet Goethe, his German contemporary, said, "The sense of mystery in the grasp of despair is at moments almost Shakespearean."

DOROTHY WELLESLEY

LINES WRITTEN BENEATH AN ELM IN THE CHURCHYARD OF HARROW

Spot of my youth ! whose hoary branches sigh,
Swept by the breeze that fans thy cloudless sky ;
Where now alone I muse, who oft have trod,
With those I loved, thy soft and verdant sod ;
With those who, scatter'd far, perchance deplore,
Like me, the happy scenes they knew before :
Oh ! as I trace again thy winding hill,
Mine eyes admire, my heart adores thee still.
Thou drooping Elm ! beneath whose boughs I lay,
And frequent mused the twilight hours away ;
Where, as they once were wont, my limbs recline,
But, ah ! without the thoughts which then were
    mine :
How do thy branches, moaning to the blast,
Invite the bosom to recall the past,
And seem to whisper, as they gently swell,
" Take, while thou canst, a lingering, last fare-
    well ! "

When fate shall chill, at length this fever'd breast,
And calm its cares and passions into rest,
Oft have I thought, 'twould soothe my dying
hour,—
If aught may soothe when life resigns her power,—
To know some humbler grave, some narrow cell,
Would hide my bosom where it loved to dwell ;
With this fond dream, methinks, 'twere sweet to
die—
And here it linger'd, here my heart might lie ;
Here might I sleep where all my hopes arose,
Scene of my youth, and couch of my repose ;
For ever stretch'd beneath this mantling shade,
Press'd by the turf where once my childhood
play'd ;
Wrapt by the soil that veils the spot I loved,
Mix'd with the earth o'er which my footsteps
moved ;
Blest by the tongues that charm'd my youthful ear,
Mourn'd by the few my soul acknowledged here ;
Deplored by those in early days allied,
And unremember'd by the world beside.

September 2, 1807

HARROW SCHOOL IN 1802
Engraving

WHEN WE TWO PARTED

WHEN we two parted
In silence and tears,
Half broken-hearted
To sever for years,
Pale grew thy cheek and cold,
Colder thy kiss ;
Truly that hour foretold
Sorrow to this.

BYRON
Miniature by James Holmes 1817

By courtesy of the Headmaster of Harrow School

The dew of the morning
Sunk chill on my brow—
It felt like the warning
Of what I feel now.
Thy vows are all broken,
And light is thy fame ;
I hear thy name spoken,
And share in its shame.

They name thee before me,
A knell to mine ear ;
A shudder comes o'er me—
Why wert thou so dear ?
They know not I knew thee,
Who knew thee too well :—
Long, long shall I rue thee.
Too deeply to tell.

In secret we met—
In silence I grieve,
That thy heart could forget,
Thy spirit deceive.
If I should meet thee
After long years,
How should I greet thee ?—
With silence and tears.

1808

LINES INSCRIBED UPON A CUP
FORMED FROM A SKULL

START not—nor deem my spirit fled :
In me behold the only skull,
From which, unlike a living head,
Whatever flows is never dull.

I lived, I loved, I quaff'd, like thee ;
I died : let earth my bones resign :
Fill up—thou canst not injure me ;
The worm hath fouler lips than thine.

Better to hold the sparkling grape,
Than nurse the earth-worm's slimy brood ;
And circle in the goblet's shape
The drink of gods, than reptile's food.

Where once my wit, perchance, hath shone,
In aid of others' let me shine ;
And when, alas ! our brains are gone,
What nobler substitute than wine ?

Quaff while thou canst : another race,
When thou and thine like me are sped,
May rescue thee from earth's embrace,
And rhyme and revel with the dead.

Why not ? since through life's little day
Our heads such sad effects produce ;
Redeem'd from worms and wasting clay,
This chance is theirs, to be of use.

Newstead Abbey 1808

From
THE VISION OF JUDGMENT

SAINT PETER sat by the celestial gate :
  His keys were rusty, and the lock was dull,
So little trouble had been given of late ;
  Not that the place by any means was full,
But since the Gallic era " eighty-eight "
  The devils had ta'en a longer, stronger pull,
And " a pull altogether," as they say
At sea—which drew most souls another way.

*   *   *

The guardian seraphs had retired on high,
  Finding their charges past all care below ;
Terrestrial business fill'd nought in the sky
  Save the recording angel's black bureau ;
Who found, indeed, the facts to multiply
  With such rapidity of vice and woe,
That he had stripp'd off both his wings in quills,
And yet was in arrear of human ills.

*   *   *

God help us all ! God help me too ! I am,
  God knows, as helpless as the devil can wish,
And not a whit more difficult to damn,
  Than is to bring to land a late-hook'd fish,
Or to the butcher to purvey the lamb ;
  Not that I'm fit for such a noble dish,
As one day will be that immortal fry
Of almost everybody born to die.

Canto III.   Stanzas XXI–XXV

There was a sound of revelry by night,
And Belgium's capital had gather'd then
Her Beauty and her Chivalry, and bright
The lamps shone o'er fair women and brave men;
A thousand hearts beat happily ; and when
Music arose with its voluptuous swell,
Soft eyes look'd love to eyes which spake again,
And all went merry as a marriage-bell ;
But hush ! hark ! a deep sound strikes like a
     rising knell !

Did ye not hear it ?—No ; 'twas but the wind
Or the car rattling o'er the stony street ;
On with the dance ! let joy be unconfined ;
No sleep till morn, when Youth and Pleasure meet
To chase the glowing Hours with flying feet—
But, hark !—that heavy sound breaks in once more.
As if the clouds its echo would repeat ;
And nearer, clearer, deadlier than before !
Arm ! Arm ! it is—it is—the cannon's opening
     roar !

Within a window'd niche of that high hall
Sate Brunswick's fated chieftain ; he did hear
That sound the first amidst the festival,

And caught its tone with Death's prophetic ear ;
And when they smiled because he deem'd it near,
His heart more truly knew that peal too well
Which stretch'd his father on a bloody bier.
And roused the vengeance blood alone could
    quell :
He rush'd into the field, and, foremost fighting,
    fell.

Ah ! then and there was hurrying to and fro,
And gathering tears, and tremblings of distress,
And cheeks all pale, which but an hour ago
Blush'd at the praise of their own loveliness ;
And there were sudden partings, such as press
The life from out young hearts, and choking sighs
Which ne'er might be repeated ; who could guess
If ever more should meet those mutual eyes,
Since upon night so sweet such awful morn could
    rise !

And there was mounting in hot haste : the steed,
The mustering squadron, and the clattering car,
Went pouring forward with impetuous speed,
And swiftly forming in the ranks of war ;
And the deep thunder peal on peal afar ;
And near, the beat of the alarming drum
Roused up the soldier ere the morning star ;
While throng'd the citizens with terror dumb,
Or whispering, with white lips—" The foe ! They
    come ! they come ! "

I have not loved the world, nor the world me ;
I have not flatter'd its rank breath, nor bow'd
To its idolatries a patient knee,—
Nor coin'd my cheek to smiles,—nor cried aloud
In worship of an echo ; in the crowd
They could not deem me one of such ; I stood
Among them, but not of them ; in a shroud
Of thoughts which were not their thoughts, and
    still could,
Had I not filed my mind, which thus itself
    subdued.

Canto IV.   Stanzas XXX–XXXI

There is a tomb in Arqua ;—rear'd in air,
Pillar'd in their sarcophagus, repose
The bones of Laura's lover ; here repair
Many familiar with his well-sung woes,
The pilgrims of his genius. He arose
To raise a language, and his land reclaim
From the dull yoke of her barbaric foes :
Watering the tree which bears his lady's name
With his melodious tears, he gave himself to fame.

They keep his dust in Arqua, where he died ;
The mountain-village where his latter days
Went down the vale of years ; and 'tis their
    pride—
An honest pride—and let it be their praise,
To offer to the passing stranger's gaze

20

CHILDE HAROLD

Facsimile of original draft for Canto IV, stanza XCI

His mansion and his sepulchre ; both plain
And venerably simple, such as raise
A feeling more accordant with his strain
Than if a pyramid form'd his monumental fane.

Canto IV. Stanzas XLIV–XLIX

Wandering in youth, I traced the path of him,
The Roman friend of Rome's least-mortal mind,
The friend of Tully : as my bark did skim
The bright blue waters with a fanning wind,
Came Megara before me, and behind
Ægina lay, Piræus on the right,
And Corinth on the left ; I lay reclined
Along the prow, and saw all these unite
In ruin, even as he had seen the desolate sight ;

For Time hath not rebuilt them, but uprear'd
Barbaric dwellings on their shatter'd site,
Which only make more mourn'd and more
      endear'd
The few last rays of their far-scatter'd light,
And the crush'd relics of their vanish'd might.
The Roman saw these tombs in his own age,
These sepulchres of cities, which excite
Sad wonder, and his yet surviving page
The moral lesson bears, drawn from such
      pilgrimage.

That page is now before me, and on mine
His country's ruin added to the mass
Of perish'd states he mourn'd in their decline,

And I in desolation : all that *was*
Of them destruction *is* ; and now, alas !
Rome—Rome imperial, bows her to the storm,
In the same dust and blackness, and we pass
The skeleton of her Titanic form,
Wrecks of another world, whose ashes still are
    warm.

Yet, Italy ! through every other land
Thy wrongs should ring, and shall, from side to
    side ;
Mother of Arts ! as once of arms ; thy hand
Was then our guardian, and is still our guide ;
Parent of our Religion ! whom the wide
Nations have knelt to for the keys of heaven !
Europe, repentant of her parricide,
Shall yet redeem thee, and, all backward driven,
Roll the barbarian tide, and sue to be forgiven.

But Arno wins us to the fair white walls,
Where the Etrurian Athens claims and keeps
A softer feeling for her fairy halls.
Girt by her theatre of hills, she reaps
Her corn, and wine, and oil, and Plenty leaps
To laughing life, with her redundant horn.
Along the banks where smiling Arno sweeps
Was modern Luxury of Commerce born,
And buried Learning rose, redeem'd to a new
    morn.

There, too, the Goddess loves in stone, and fills
The air around with beauty ; we inhale
The ambrosial aspect, which, beheld, instils

Part of its immortality ; the veil
Of heaven is half undrawn ; within the pale
We stand, and in that form and face behold
What mind can make, when Nature's self would
    fail ;
And to the fond idolaters of old
Envy the innate flash which such a soul could
    mould.

Canto IV. Stanzas LIV–LX

In Santa Croce's holy precincts lie
Ashes which make it holier, dust which is
Even in itself an immortality,
Though there were nothing save the past, and this,
The particle of those sublimities
Which have relapsed to chaos :—here repose
Angelo's, Alfieri's bones, and his,
The starry Galileo, with his woes ;
Here Machiavelli's earth return'd to whence it
    rose.

These are four minds, which, like the elements,
Might furnish forth creation :—Italy !
Time, which hath wrong'd thee with ten thousand
    rents
Of thine imperial garment, shall deny,
And hath denied, to every other sky,
Spirits which soar from ruin :—thy decay
Is still impregnate with divinity,

BYRON
Mezzotint after an oil painting by Westall 1814

Which gilds it with revivifying ray ;
Such as the great of yore, Canova is to-day.

But where repose the all Etruscan three—
Dante, and Petrarch, and, scarce less than they,
The Bard of Prose, creative spirit ! he
Of the Hundred Tales of love—where did they lay
Their bones, distinguish'd from our common clay
In death as life ? Are they resolved to dust,
And have their country's marbles nought to say ?
Could not her quarries furnish forth one bust ?
Did they not to her breast their filial earth intrust ?

Ungrateful Florence ! Dante sleeps afar,
Like Scipio, buried by the upbraiding shore ;
Thy factions, in their worse than civil war,
Proscribed the bard whose name for evermore
Their children's children would in vain adore
With the remorse of ages ; and the crown
Which Petrarch's laureate brow supremely wore,
Upon a far and foreign soil had grown,
His life, his fame, his grave, though rifled—not
    thine own.

Boccaccio to his parent earth bequeath'd
His dust,—and lies it not her Great among,
With many a sweet and solemn requiem breathed
O'er him who form'd the Tuscan's siren tongue?
That music in itself, whose sounds are song,
The poetry of speech ? No ;—even his tomb
Uptorn, must bear the hyæna bigot's wrong,
No more amidst the meaner dead find room,
Nor claim a passing sigh, because it told for *whom* !

And Santa Croce wants their mighty dust ;
Yet for this want more noted, as of yore
The Cæsar's pageant, shorn of Brutus' bust,
Did but of Rome's best Son remind her more :
Happier Ravenna ! on thy hoary shore,
Fortress of falling empire ! honour'd sleeps
The immortal exile ;—Arqua, too, her store
Of tuneful relics proudly claims and keeps,
While Florence vainly begs her banish'd dead
    and weeps.

What is her pyramid of precious stones ?
Of porphyry, jasper, agate, and all hues
Of gem and marble, to encrust the bones
Of merchant-dukes ? the momentary dews
Which, sparkling to the twilight stars, infuse
Freshness in the green turf that wraps the dead,
Whose names are mausoleums of the Muse,
Are gently prest with far more reverent tread
Than ever paced the slab which paves the princely
    head.

Canto IV.   Stanzas LXXVIII–LXXIX

Oh Rome ! my country ! city of the soul !
The orphans of the heart must turn to thee,
Lone mother of dead empires ! and control
In their shut breasts their petty misery.
What are our woes and sufferance ? Come and see
The cypress, hear the owl, and plod your way
O'er steps of broken thrones and temples, Ye !

27

Whose agonies are evils of a day—
A world is at our feet as fragile as our clay.

The Niobe of nations ! there she stands,
Childless and crownless, in her voiceless woe ;
An empty urn within her wither'd hands,
Whose holy dust was scatter'd long ago :
The Scipios' tomb contains no ashes now ;
The very sepulchres lie tenantless
Of their heroic dwellers : dost thou flow,
Old Tiber ! through a marble wilderness ?
Rise, with thy yellow waves, and mantle her
  distress.

Canto IV.   Stanzas XCIX–CIII

There is a stern round tower of other days,
Firm as a fortress, with its fence of stone,
Such as an army's baffled strength delays,
Standing with half its battlements alone,
And with two thousand years of ivy grown,
The garland of eternity, where wave
The green leaves over all by time o'erthrown ;—
What was this tower of strength ? within its cave
What treasure lay so lock'd, so hid ?—A woman's
  grave.

But who was she, the lady of the dead,
Tomb'd in a palace ? Was she chaste and fair ?
Worthy a king's—or more—a Roman's bed ?
What race of chiefs and heroes did she bear ?
What daughter of her beauties was the heir ?

How lived—how loved—how died she? Was
    she not
So honour'd—and conspicuously there,
Where meaner relics must not dare to rot,
Placed to commemorate a more than mortal lot?

Was she as those who love their lords, or they
Who love the lords of others? such have been
Even in the olden time, Rome's annals say.
Was she a matron of Cornelia's mien,
Or the light air of Egypt's graceful queen,
Profuse of joy—or 'gainst it did she war,
Inveterate in virtue? Did she lean
To the soft side of the heart, or wisely bar
Love from amongst her griefs?—for such the
    affections are.

Perchance she died in youth: it may be, bow'd
With foes far heavier than the ponderous tomb
That weigh'd upon her gentle dust, a cloud
Might gather o'er her beauty, and a gloom
In her dark eye, prophetic of the doom
Heaven gives its favourites—early death; yet shed
A sunset charm around her, and illume
With hectic light, the Hesperus of the dead,
Of her consuming cheek the autumnal leaf-like
    red.

Perchance she died in age—surviving all,
Charms, kindred, children—with the silver gray
On her long tresses, which might yet recall,
It may be, still a something of the day
When they were braided, and her proud array

And lovely form were envied, praised, and eyed
By Rome—but whither would Conjecture stray?
Thus much alone we know—Metella died
The wealthiest Roman's wife : Behold his love
    or pride !

Canto IV.   Stanza CX

Tully was not so eloquent as thou,
Thou nameless column with the buried base !
What are the laurels of the Cæsar's brow ?
Crown me with ivy from his dwelling-place.
Whose arch or pillar meets me in the face,
Titus or Trajan's ? No—'tis that of Time :
Triumph, arch, pillar, all he doth displace,
Scoffing ; and apostolic statues climb
To crush the imperial urn, whose ashes slept
    sublime. . . .

Canto IV.   Stanzas CXL–CXLI

I see before me the Gladiator lie :
He leans upon his hand—his manly brow
Consents to death, but conquers agony,
And his droop'd head sinks gradually low—
And through his side the last drops, ebbing slow
From the red gash, fall heavy, one by one,
Like the first of a thunder-shower ; and now
The arena swims around him—he is gone,
Ere ceased the inhuman shout which hail'd the
    wretch who won.

30

He heard it, but he heeded not—his eyes
Were with his heart, and that was far away :
He reck'd not of the life he lost nor prize,
But where his rude hut by the Danube lay,
There were his young barbarians all at play,
There was their Dacian mother—he, their sire,
Butcher'd to make a Roman holiday—
All this rush'd with his blood—Shall he expire
And unavenged ?—Arise ! ye Goths, and glut
    your ire !

Canto IV. Stanzas CLXXVII–CLXXIX

Oh ! that the Desert were my dwelling-place,
With one fair Spirit for my minister,
That I might all forget the human race,
And, hating no one, love but only her !
Ye Elements !—in whose ennobling stir
I feel myself exalted—Can ye not
Accord me such a being ? Do I err
In deeming such inhabit many a spot ?
Though with them to converse can rarely be our
    lot.

There is a pleasure in the pathless woods,
There is a rapture on the lonely shore,
There is society, where none intrudes,
By the deep Sea, and music in its roar :
I love not Man the less, but Nature more,
From these our interviews, in which I steal
From all I may be, or have been before,

To mingle with the Universe, and feel
What I can ne'er express, yet can not all conceal.

Roll on, thou deep and dark blue Ocean—roll !
Ten thousand fleets sweep over thee in vain ;
Man marks the earth with ruin—his control
Stops with the shore ;—upon the watery plain
The wrecks are all thy deed, nor doth remain
A shadow of man's ravage, save his own,
When, for a moment, like a drop of rain,
He sinks into thy depths with bubbling groan,
Without a grave, unknell'd, uncoffin'd, and
  unknown.

Canto IV. Stanza CLXXXIV

And I have loved thee, Ocean ! and my joy
Of youthful sports was on thy breast to be
Borne, like thy bubbles, onward : from a boy
I wanton'd with thy breakers—they to me
Were a delight ; and if the freshening sea
Made them a terror—'twas a pleasing fear,
For I was as it were a child of thee,
And trusted to thy billows far and near,
And laid my hand upon thy mane—as I do here.

1912

BYRON
Engraving after a drawing by Harlow 1815

From
THE CORSAIR

Canto I.　Stanza I

" O'ER the glad waters of the dark blue sea,
Our thoughts as boundless, and our souls as free,
Far as the breeze can bear, the billows foam,
Survey our empire, and behold our home !
These are our realms, no limits to their sway—
Our flag the sceptre all who meet obey.
Ours the wild life in tumult still to range
From toil to rest, and joy in every change.
Oh, who can tell ? not thou, luxurious slave !
Whose soul would sicken o'er the heaving wave ;
Not thou, vain lord of wantonness and ease !
Whom slumber soothes not—pleasure cannot
　　please—
Oh, who can tell, save he whose heart hath tried,
And danced in triumph o'er the waters wide,
The exulting sense—the pulse's maddening play,
That thrills the wanderer of that trackless way ?
That for itself can woo the approaching fight,
And turn what some deem danger to delight ;
That seeks what cravens shun with more than
　　zeal,
And where the feebler faint can only feel—
Feel—to the rising bosom's inmost core,
Its hope awaken and its spirit soar ?
No dread of death if with us die our foes—
Save that it seems even duller than repose :
Come when it will—we snatch the life of life—

When lost—what recks it but disease or strife?
Let him who crawls enamour'd of decay,
Cling to his couch, and sicken years away :
Heave his thick breath, and shake his palsied
    head ;
Ours—the fresh turf, and not the feverish bed.
While gasp by gasp he falters forth his soul,
Ours with one pang—one bound—escapes control.
His corse may boast its urn and narrow cave,
And they who loath'd his life may gild his grave ;
Ours are the tears, though few, sincerely shed,
When Ocean shrouds and sepulchres our dead.
For us, even banquets fond regret supply
In the red cup that crowns our memory ;
And the brief epitaph in danger's day,
When those who win at length divide the prey,
And cry, Remembrance saddening o'er each brow,
How had the brave who fell exulted now ! "

1814

STANZAS FOR MUSIC

THERE's not a joy the world can give like that it
    takes away,
When the glow of early thought declines in
    feeling's dull decay ;
'Tis not on youth's smooth cheek the blush
    alone, which fades so fast,
But the tender bloom of heart is gone, ere youth
    itself be past.

Then the few whose spirits float above the wreck
    of happiness
Are driven o'er the shoals of guilt or ocean of
    excess :
The magnet of their course is gone, or only points
    in vain
The shore to which their shiver'd sail shall never
    stretch again.

Then the mortal coldness of the soul like death
    itself comes down ;
It cannot feel for others' woes, it dare not dream
    its own ;
That heavy chill has frozen o'er the fountain of
    our tears,
And though the eye may sparkle still, 'tis where
    the ice appears.

Though wit may flash from fluent lips, and
    mirth distract the breast,
Through midnight hours that yield no more
    their former hope of rest ;
'Tis but as ivy-leaves around the ruin'd turret
    wreath,
All green and wildly fresh without, but worn and
    grey beneath.

Oh, could I feel as I have felt,—or be what I
    have been,
Or weep as I could once have wept, o'er many a
    vanish'd scene ;
As springs in deserts found seem sweet, all brackish
    though they be,
So, midst the wither'd waste of life, those tears
    would flow to me.

1815

STANZAS FOR MUSIC

There be none of Beauty's daughters
With a magic like thee ;
And like music on the waters
Is thy sweet voice to me :
When, as if its sound were causing
The charmed ocean's pausing,
The waves lie still and gleaming,
And the lull'd winds seem dreaming.

And the midnight moon is weaving
Her bright chain o'er the deep ;
Whose breast is gently heaving,
As an infant's asleep :
So the spirit bows before thee,
To listen and adore thee ;
With a full but soft emotion,
Like the swell of Summer's ocean.

1815

ANNABELLA MILBANKE (later LADY BYRON)
in her Twentieth year
Miniature by Hayter

SHE WALKS IN BEAUTY

SHE walks in beauty, like the night
Of cloudless climes and starry skies ;
And all that's best of dark and bright
Meet in her aspect and her eyes :
Thus mellow'd to that tender light
Which heaven to gaudy day denies.

One shade the more, one ray the less,
Had half impair'd the nameless grace
Which waves in every raven tress,
Or softly lightens o'er her face ;
Where thoughts serenely sweet express
How pure, how dear their dwelling-place.

And on that cheek, and o'er that brow,
So soft, so calm, yet eloquent,
The smiles that win, the tints that glow,
But tell of days in goodness spent,
A mind at peace with all below,
A heart whose love is innocent !

1815

OH ! SNATCH'D AWAY IN
BEAUTY'S BLOOM

Oh ! snatch'd away in beauty's bloom,
On thee shall press no ponderous tomb ;
But on thy turf shall roses rear
Their leaves, the earliest of the year ;
And the wild cypress wave in tender gloom :

And oft by yon blue gushing stream
Shall Sorrow lean her drooping head,
And feed deep thought with many a dream,
And lingering pause and lightly tread ;
Fond wretch ! as if her step disturb'd the dead !

Away ! we know that tears are vain,
That death nor heeds nor hears distress :
Will this unteach us to complain ?
Or make one mourner weep the less ?
And thou—who tell'st me to forget,
Thy looks are wan, thine eyes are wet.

1815.

THE DESTRUCTION OF SENNACHERIB

THE Assyrian came down like the wolf on the fold,
And his cohorts were gleaming in purple and gold ;
And the sheen of their spears was like stars on
    the sea,
When the blue wave rolls nightly on deep Galilee.

Like the leaves of the forest when Summer is green,
That host with their banners at sunset were seen :
Like the leaves of the forest when Autumn hath
    blown,
That host on the morrow lay wither'd and strown.

For the Angel of Death spread his wings on the
    blast,
And breathed in the face of the foe as he pass'd ;
And the eyes of the sleepers wax'd deadly and
    chill,
And their hearts but once heaved, and for ever
    grew still !

And there lay the steed with his nostril all wide,
But through it there roll'd not the breath of his
    pride :
And the foam of his gasping lay white on the turf,
And cold as the spray of the rock-beating surf.

And there lay the rider distorted and pale,
With the dew on his brow, and the rust on his
    mail ;

BYRON AND HIS SHIP
Engraving after an oil painting by Sanders

And the tents were all silent, the banners alone,
The lances unlifted, the trumpet unblown.

And the widows of Ashur are loud in their wail,
And the idols are broke in the temple of Baal ;
And the might of the Gentile, unsmote by the
    sword,
Hath melted like snow in the glance of the Lord !

1815

BYRON
Engraving after an oil painting by Phillips

THE HON. MRS. LEIGH
Byron's half-sister
Engraving after a miniature by Holmes 1833

SONNET ON CHILLON

ETERNAL Spirit of the chainless Mind !
Brightest in dungeons, Liberty, thou art !
For there thy habitation is the heart—
The heart which love of thee alone can bind ;
And when thy sons to fetters are consign'd—
To fetters, and the damp vault's dayless gloom,
Their country conquers with their martyrdom,
And Freedom's fame finds wings on every wind.
Chillon ! thy prison is a holy place,
And thy sad floor an altar—for 'twas trod,
Until his very steps have left a trace
Worn, as if thy cold pavement were a sod,
By Bonnivard !—May none those marks efface !
For they appeal from tyranny to God.

1816

STANZAS TO AUGUSTA

When all around grew drear and dark,
  And reason half withheld her ray—
And hope but shed a dying spark
  Which more misled my lonely way ;

In that deep midnight of the mind,
  And that internal strife of heart,
When dreading to be deem'd too kind,
  The weak despair—the cold depart ;

When fortune changed—and love fled far,
  And hatred's shafts flew thick and fast,
Thou wert the solitary star
  Which rose and set not to the last.

Oh ! blest be thine unbroken light !
  That watch'd me as a seraph's eye,
And stood between me and the night,
  For ever shining sweetly nigh.

And when the cloud upon us came,
  Which strove to blacken o'er thy ray—
Then purer spread its gentle flame,
  And dash'd the darkness all away.

Still may thy spirit dwell on mine,
  And teach it what to brave or brook—
There's more in one soft word of thine
  Than in the world's defied rebuke.

Thou stood'st, as stands a lovely tree,
    That still unbroke, though gently bent,
Still waves with fond fidelity
    Its boughs above a monument.

The winds might rend—the skies might pour,
    But there thou wert—and still wouldst be
Devoted in the stormiest hour
    To shed thy weeping leaves o'er me.

But thou and thine shall know no blight,
    Whatever fate on me may fall ;
For heaven in sunshine will requite
    The kind—and thee the most of all.

Then let the ties of baffled love
    Be broken—thine will never break ;
Thy heart can feel—but will not move ;
    Thy soul, though soft, will never shake.

And these, when all was lost beside,
    Were found and still are fix'd in thee ;—
And bearing still a breast so tried,
    Earth is no desert—ev'n to me.

1816

BYRON IN ALBANIAN DRESS
Oil painting by Phillips

By courtesy of the Countess of Lovelace

CHURCHILL'S GRAVE
A fact literally rendered

I STOOD beside the grave of him who blazed
The comet of a season, and I saw
The humblest of all sepulchres, and gazed
With not the less of sorrow and of awe
On that neglected turf and quiet stone,
With name no clearer than the names unknown,
Which lay unread around it ; and I ask'd
The Gardener of that ground, why it might be
That for this plant strangers his memory task'd
Through the thick deaths of half a century ;
And thus he answer'd—" Well, I do not know
Why frequent travellers turn to pilgrims so ;
He died before my day of Sextonship,
And I had not the digging of this grave."
And is this all ? I thought,—and do we rip
The veil of Immortality ? and crave
I know not what of honour and of light
Through unborn ages, to endure this blight ?
So soon, and so successless ? As I said,
The Architect of all on which we tread,
For Earth is but a tombstone, did essay
To extricate remembrance from the clay,
Whose minglings might confuse a Newton's
        thought,
Were it not that all life must end in one,
Of which we are but dreamers ;—as he caught
As 'twere the twilight of a former Sun,
Thus spoke he,—" I believe the man of whom
You wot, who lies in this selected tomb,

Was a most famous writer in his day,
And therefore travellers step from out their way
To pay him honour,—and myself whate'er
Your honour pleases,"—then most pleased I shook
From out my pocket's avaricious nook
Some certain coins of silver, which as 'twere
Perforce I gave this man, though I could spare
So much but inconveniently :—Ye smile,
I see ye, ye profane ones ! all the while,
Because my homely phrase the truth would tell.
You are the fools, not I—for I did dwell
With a deep thought, and with a soften'd eye,
On that Old Sexton's natural homily,
In which there was Obscurity and Fame,—
The Glory and the Nothing of a Name.

Diodati 1816

BYRON AT THE VILLA DIODATI

Mezzotint after an oil painting c. 1816

BYRON
Silhouette by Mrs. Leigh Hunt

TO THOMAS MOORE

My boat is on the shore,
And my bark is on the sea ;
But, before I go, Tom Moore,
Here's a double health to thee !

Here's a sigh to those who love me,
And a smile to those who hate ;
And, whatever sky's above me,
Here's a heart for every fate.

Though the ocean roar around me,
Yet it still shall bear me on ;
Though a desert should surround me,
It hath springs that may be won.

Were't the last drop in the well,
As I gasp'd upon the brink,
Ere my fainting spirit fell,
'Tis to thee that I would drink.

Was that water, as this wine,
The libation I would pour
Should be—peace with thine and mine.
And a health to thee, Tom Moore.

July, 1817

SO, WE'LL GO NO MORE A ROVING

So, we'll go no more a roving
  So late into the night,
Though the heart be still as loving,
  And the moon be still as bright.

For the sword outwears its sheath,
  And the soul wears out the breast,
And the heart must pause to breathe,
  And love itself have rest.

Though the night was made for loving,
  And the day returns too soon,
Yet we'll go no more a roving
  By the light of the moon.

1817

MOCENIGO PALACE

The Venetian palace where Byron lived between 1817-1819
From a drawing by Lady Eastlake

From
MANFRED

THE stars are forth, the moon above the tops
Of the snow-shining mountains.—Beautiful !
I linger yet with Nature, for the night
Hath been to me a more familiar face
Than that of man ; and in her starry shade
Of dim and solitary loveliness,
I learn'd the language of another world.
I do remember me, that in my youth,
When I was wandering,—upon such a night
I stood within the Coliseum's wall,
Midst the chief relics of almighty Rome ;
The trees which grew along the broken arches
Waved dark in the blue midnight, and the stars
Shone through the rents of ruin ; from afar
The watchdog bay'd beyond the Tiber ; and
More near from out the Cæsars' palace came
The owl's long cry, and, interruptedly,
Of distant sentinels the fitful song
Begun and died upon the gentle wind.
Some cypresses beyond the time-worn breach
Appear'd to skirt the horizon, yet they stood
Within a bowshot—Where the Cæsars dwelt,
And dwell the tuneless birds of night, amidst
A grove which springs through levell'd battlements,
And twines its roots with the imperial hearths,
Ivy usurps the laurel's place of growth ;—
But the gladiators' bloody Circus stands,
A noble wreck in ruinous perfection !
While Cæsar's chambers, and the Augustan halls,
56

Grovel on earth in indistinct decay.—
And thou didst shine, thou rolling moon, upon
All this, and cast a wide and tender light,
Which soften'd down the hoar austerity
Of rugged desolation, and fill'd up,
As 'twere anew, the gaps of centuries ;
Leaving that beautiful which still was so,
And making that which was not, till the place
Became religion, and the heart ran o'er
With silent worship of the great of old !—
The dead, but sceptred sovereigns, who still rule
Our spirits from their urns.

1817

TO MR. MURRAY

STRAHAN, Tonson, Lintot of the times,
Patron and publisher of rhymes,
For thee the bard up Pindus climbs,
       My Murray.

To thee, with hope and terror dumb,
The unfledged MS. authors come ;
Thou printest all—and sellest some—
       My Murray.

Upon thy table's baize so green
The last new Quarterly is seen,—
But where is thy new Magazine,
       My Murray ?

Along thy sprucest bookshelves shine
The works thou deemest most divine—
The " Art of Cookery," and mine,
       My Murray.

Tours, Travels, Essays, too, I wist,
And Sermons to thy mill bring grist ;
And then thou hast the " Navy List,"
       My Murray.

And Heaven forbid I should conclude
Without " the Board of Longitude,"
Although this narrow paper would,
       My Murray !

Venice, March 25, 1818

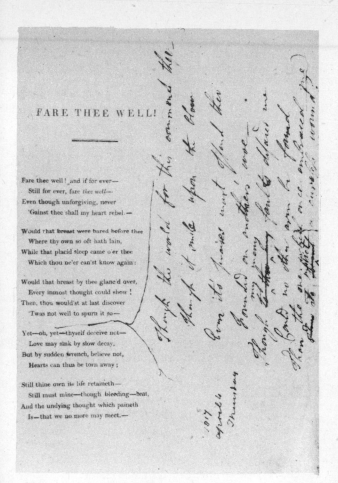

PROOF OF *FARE THEE WELL*
Quatrain in Byron's handwriting dated 4th April, 1817

STANZAS TO THE PO

River, that rollest by the ancient walls,
Where dwells the lady of my love, when she
Walks by thy brink, and there perchance recalls
A faint and fleeting memory of me ;

What if thy deep and ample stream should be
A mirror of my heart, where she may read
The thousand thoughts I now betray to thee,
Wild as thy wave, and headlong as thy speed !

What do I say—a mirror of my heart ?
Are not thy waters sweeping, dark, and strong ?
Such as my feelings were and are, thou art ;
And such as thou art were my passions long.

Time may have somewhat tamed them,—not for
    ever ;
Thou overflow'st thy banks, and not for aye
The bosom overboils, congenial river !
Thy floods subside, and mine have sunk away.

But left long wrecks behind, and now again,
Born in our old unchanged career, we move ;
Thou tendest wildly onwards to the main,
And I—to loving *one* I should not love.

The current I behold will sweep beneath
Her native walls and murmur at her feet ;
Her eyes will look on thee, when she shall breathe
The twilight air, unharm'd by summer's heat.

THE COUNTESS GUICCIOLI
Engraved by Count D'Orsay from his own drawing 1839

She will look on thee,—I have look'd on thee,
Full of that thought ; and, from that moment,
   ne'er
Thy waters could I dream of, name, or see,
Without the inseparable sigh for her !

Her bright eyes will be imaged in thy stream,—
Yes ! they will meet the wave I gaze on now :
Mine cannot witness, even in a dream,
That happy wave repass me in its flow !

The wave that bears my tears returns no more:
Will she return by whom that wave shall sweep ?
Both tread thy banks, both wander on thy shore,
I by thy source, she by the dark-blue deep.

But that which keepeth us apart is not
Distance, nor depth of wave, nor space of earth,
But the distraction of a various lot,
As various as the climates of our birth.

A stranger loves the lady of the land,
Born far beyond the mountains, but his blood
Is all meridian, as if never fann'd
By the black wind that chills the polar flood,

My blood is all meridian ; were it not,
I had not left my clime, nor should I be,
In spite of tortures, ne'er to be forgot,
A slave again of love,—at least of thee.

'Tis vain to struggle—let me perish young—
Live as I lived, and love as I have loved ;
To dust if I return, from dust I sprung,
And then, at least, my heart can ne'er be moved.

K. Seymour, del.

London, Pub. by Knight & Lacey, Paternoster Row, 1825.

I. Clark sculp.

Lord Byron's House Missolonghi

By courtesy of Sir John Murray

Canto III. Stanza LXXXVI

IN France, for instance, he would write a chanson;
In England a six canto quarto tale;
In Spain, he'd make a ballad or romance on
The last war—much the same in Portugal;
In Germany, the Pegasus he'd prance on
Would be old Goethe's—(see what says De Staël);
In Italy he'd ape the " Trecentisti " ;
In Greece, he'd sing some sort of hymn like this
      t'ye :

The isles of Greece, the isles of Greece !
Where burning Sappho loved and sung,
Where grew the arts of war and peace,—
Where Delos rose, and Phœbus sprung !
Eternal summer gilds them yet,
But all, except their sun, is set.

The Scian and the Teian muse,
The hero's harp, the lover's lute,
Have found the fame your shores refuse ;
Their place of birth alone is mute
To sounds which echo further west
Than your sires' " Islands of the Blest."

The mountains look on Marathon—
And Marathon looks on the sea ;
And musing there an hour alone,
I dream'd that Greece might still be free ;

For standing on the Persians' grave,
I could not deem myself a slave.

A king sate on the rocky brow
Which looks o'er sea-born Salamis ;
And ships, by thousands, lay below,
And men in nations ;—all were his !
He counted them at break of day—
And when the sun set where were they ?

And where are they ? and where art thou,
My country ? On thy voiceless shore
The heroic lay is tuneless now—
The heroic bosom beats no more !
And must thy lyre, so long divine,
Degenerate into hands like mine ?

'Tis something, in the dearth of fame,
Though link'd among a fetter'd race,
To feel at least a patriot's shame,
Even as I sing, suffuse my face ;
For what is left the poet here ?
For Greeks a blush—for Greece a tear.

Must *we* but weep o'er days more blest ?
Must *we* but blush ?—Our fathers bled.
Earth ! render back from out thy breast
A remnant of our Spartan dead !
Of the three hundred grant but three,
To make a new Thermopylæ !

What, silent still ? and silent all ?
Ah ! no ;—the voices of the dead
Sound like a distant torrent's fall,

Genoa May 19th 1823

Dear Sir — I will thank you very much to present to
or obtain for the bearer — a print from the mini-
ature you drew of me in 2015. — I prefer that
likeness to any which has been done of me by any artist
whatever. — — My sister Mrs Leigh — or the
Honble Douglas Kinnaird — will pay you the
price of the engraving. — — am yours

Noel Byron

To

— Holmes Esqre

BYRON
The poet's favourite portrait
Engraving after a miniature by Holmes 1835

And answer, " Let one living head,
But one arise,—we come, we come ! "
'Tis but the living who are dumb.

In vain—in vain : strike other chords ;
Fill high the cup with Samian wine !
Leave battles to the Turkish hordes,
And shed the blood of Scio's vine !
Hark ! rising to the ignoble call—
How answers each bold Bacchanal !

You have the Pyrrhic dance as yet,
Where is the Pyrrhic phalanx gone ?
Of two such lessons, why forget
The nobler and the manlier one ?
You have the letters Cadmus gave—
Think ye he meant them for a slave ?

Fill high the bowl with Samian wine !
We will not think of themes like these !
It made Anacreon's song divine :
He served—but served Polycrates—
A tyrant ; but our masters then
Were still, at least, our countrymen.

The tyrant of the Chersonese
Was freedom's best and bravest friend ;
That tyrant was Miltiades !
Oh ! that the present hour would lend
Another despot of the kind !
Such chains as his were sure to bind.

make Hamlet (or Diggory) "act mad"
in a strait waistcoat — as trammel
my buffoonery — if I am to be a buffoon
their gestures and my thoughts would only
be pitiably absurd — and ludicrously con=
=strained. — Why Man the Soul
of such writing is its' licence? — at
least the liberty of that licence if
one likes — not that one should a=
=buse it. — it is like trial by
Jury and Peerage — and Habeas Cor=
=pus — a very fine thing — but
chiefly in the reversion — because
no one wishes to be tried for the
mere pleasure of proving his possession
of the privilege. —

But a truce with these reflections. — you
are too earnest and eager about a work
never intended to be serious; — do you suppose
that I could have any intention but to
giggle and make giggle? — a playful satire

BYRON'S LETTER TO JOHN MURRAY DESCRIBING
THE INTENTION OF DON JUAN

THEY accuse me—*Me*—the present writer of
The present poem—of—I know not what—
A tendency to under-rate and scoff
At human power and virtue, and all that ;
And this they say in language rather rough.
Good God ! I wonder what they would be at !
I say no more than hath been said in Dante's
Verse, and by Solomon and by Cervantes :

By Swift, by Machiavel, by Rochefoucault,
By Fénélon, by Luther, and by Plato ;
By Tillotson, and Wesley, and Rousseau,
Who knew this life was not worth a potato.
'T is not their fault, nor mine, if this be so—
For my part, I pretend not to be Cato,
Nor even Diogenes—We live and die,
But which is best, you know no more than I.

Canto VIII. Stanzas LXV-LXVII

HE was not all alone : around him grew
A sylvan tribe of children of the chase,
Whose young, unawaken'd world was ever new,
Nor sword nor sorrow yet had left a trace
On her unwrinkled brow, nor could you view
A frown on Nature's or on human face :—
The free-born forest found and kept them free,
And fresh as is a torrent or a tree.

And tall, and strong, and swift of foot were
    they,
Beyond the dwarfing city's pale abortions,
Because their thoughts had never been the prey
Of care or gain : the green woods were their
    portions ;
No sinking spirits told them they grew grey,
No fashion made them apes of her distortions ;
Simple they were, not savage ; and their rifles,
Though very true, were not yet used for trifles.

Motion was in their days, rest in their slumbers,
And cheerfulness the handmaid of their toil ;
Nor yet too many nor too few their numbers ;
Corruption could not make their hearts her soil ;
The lust which stings, the splendour which
    encumbers,
With the free foresters divide no spoil ;
Serene, not sullen, were the solitudes
Of this unsighing people of the woods.

Canto X. Stanzas III-IV

AND wherefore this exordium ?—Why, just now,
In taking up this paltry sheet of paper,
My bosom underwent a glorious glow,
And my internal spirit cut a caper :
And though so much inferior, as I know,
To those who, by the dint of glass and vapour,
Discover stars, and sail in the wind's eye,
I wish to do as much by poesy.

In the wind's eye I have sail'd, and sail ; but for
The stars, I own my telescope is dim ;
But at the least I have shunn'd the common shore,
And leaving land far out of sight, would skim
The ocean of eternity : the roar
Of breakers has not daunted my slight, trim,
But *still* sea-worthy skiff ; and she may float
Where ships have founder'd, as doth many a boat.
                                                1818

DON JUAN.

CANTOS VI.—VII.—AND VIII.

"Dost thou think, because thou art virtuous, there shall be no more
Cakes and Ale?"—"Yes, by St. Anne; and Ginger shall be hot i'the
mouth too!"—*Twelfth Night, or What you Will.*

Shakespeare.

LONDON, 1823:

PRINTED FOR JOHN HUNT,

38, TAVISTOCK STREET, COVENT GARDEN, AND
22, OLD BOND STREET.

DON JUAN
Title page of Cantos VI - VIII, 1823

From
THE DEFORMED TRANSFORMED

BEAUTIFUL shadow
Of Thetis's boy !
Who sleeps in the meadow
Whose grass grows o'er Troy :
From the red earth, like Adam,
Thy likeness I shape,
As the being who made him,
Whose actions I ape.
Thou clay, be all glowing,
Till the rose in his cheek
Be as fair as, when blowing,
It wears its first streak !
Ye violets, I scatter,
Now turn into eyes !
And thou, sunshiny water,
Of blood take the guise !
Let these hyacinth boughs
Be his long flowing hair,
And wave o'er his brows,
As thou wavest in air !
Let his heart be this marble
I tear from the rock !
But his voice as the warble
Of birds on yon oak !
Let his flesh be the purest
Of mould, in which grew
The lily-root surest,
And drank the best dew !
Let his limbs be the lightest

Which clay can compound,
And his aspect the brightest
On earth to be found !
Elements, near me,
Be mingled and stirr'd,
Know me, and hear me,
And leap to my word !
Sunbeams, awaken
This earth's animation !
'Tis done ! He hath taken
His stand in creation !

Begun 1821, published 1824

ON THIS DAY I COMPLETE MY THIRTY-SIXTH YEAR

'Tis time this heart should be unmoved,
Since others it hath ceased to move :
Yet, though I cannot be beloved,
Still let me love !

My days are in the yellow leaf ;
The flowers and fruits of love are gone ;
The worm, the canker, and the grief
Are mine alone !

The fire that on my bosom preys
Is lone as some volcanic isle ;
No torch is kindled at its blaze—
A funeral pile !

The hope, the fear, the jealous care,
The exalted portion of the pain
And power of love, I cannot share,
But wear the chain.

But 'tis not *thus*—that 'tis not *here*—
Such thoughts should shake my soul, nor *now*,
Where glory decks the hero's bier,
Or binds his brow.

The sword, the banner, and the field,
Glory and Greece, around me see !
The Spartan, borne upon his shield,
Was not more free.

BYRON AND HIS DOG LYON
An imaginary portrait of the poet in Greece

Awake ! (not Greece—she *is* awake !)
Awake, my spirit ! Think through *whom*
Thy life-blood tracks its parent lake,
And then strike home !

Tread those reviving passions down,
Unworthy manhood !—unto thee
Indifferent should the smile or frown
Of beauty be.

If thou regret'st thy youth, *why live* ?
The land of honourable death
Is here :—up to the field, and give
Away thy breath !

Seek out—less often sought than found—
A soldier's grave, for thee the best ;
Then look around, and choose thy ground,
And take thy rest.

Missolonghi, January 22, 1824

76

INDEX OF TITLES

INDEX OF TITLES

INDEX OF FIRST LINES